SEARCHING FO

SEARCHING
for What is Not There

POEMS BY
Martin Willitts Jr

HIRAETH PRESS
DANVERS, MASSACHUSETTS

Copyright © 2013 Martin Willitts Jr

All Rights Reserved. This book may not be reproduced, in whole or in part, stored in a retrieval system, or transmitted in any form or by any means without permission from the publisher, except by a reviewer who may quote brief passages.

Cover photograph: Shutterstock
Cover and text design by Jason Kirkey

ISBN 978-0-9889430-2-5
First Edition 2013

Hiraeth Press books may be purchased for education, business or sale promotional use. For information, please write:
Special Markets
Hiraeth Press
P.O. Box 1442
Pawcatuck, CT 06379-1968

Hiraeth Press
Danvers, MA
www.hiraethpress.com

Contents

I. SPRING

3	Searching For What Is Not There
5	How We Can Change Things
6	Retribution
7	Every Spring
8	Memorial Tree
10	A Storm Is Imminent
11	Rain
12	The Beachfront
13	Spring
14	Too Soon the Clouds of Disenchanted Rains Will Be Upon Us
15	March
16	*Evening Shower at Atake and the Great Bridge*
17	Untitled (The sky refuses to rain)
18	How I Know Things Are Coming Back
19	Planting
20	Seed
22	Dutchman's Breeches

II. SUMMER

25	*Almond Branches in Bloom*
26	Garden Haikus
27	Untitled (the naiveté of the day)
28	Crickets
29	The Cricket
30	Cataracts
31	Gathering Shells
32	Untitled (The bluish butterfly bush calls to me)
33	Gardening in Georgia Clay
35	When You Left Me

36	Wildly Preaching Among Sunflowers
37	Seeing Like Never Before
38	Bloodroot
39	*Evening*
40	The Sounds of Color

III. FALL

43	September
44	Not Marble nor the Gilded Moment
45	Rose of Sharon
46	Astronomy Lessons about Love
48	Repairs and More Repairs
49	*Ile Aux Fleurs*
50	Letting Go
51	Nature
52	Ochroma Blossoms in a Rainshower
53	The Forest Is As Far or As Near As You Want It to Be
54	The River of Forgetfulness
55	Message
56	After
57	Touch Is Something We All Need

IV. WINTER

61	Trilliums
62	Trace Evidence
64	What Will Happen If We Pull Down the Empty Sky
65	Untitled (The dictionary of clouds open to the section about awakening)
66	Lasting
67	Hiroshima

70	Florida, Frost Season
71	After Winter
72	During A Long Journey
73	Extinction
74	Reaching Us
75	Singing in the Apron of Stars
76	*On The Terrace*
77	Canada Geese
78	Three Hours before New Years and Counting
79	Things We Find Instead Of Other Things
80	Acknowledgements

I.

SPRING
March, April, May

SEARCHING FOR WHAT IS NOT THERE

Looking into a lake, things are elsewhere, off
center as love when it first enters and leaves.

There is a shimmer of fish,
not where the line drops, but in an angle

frustrating as rejection. Our boat sinks and rises
heaving on the lake's chest. It takes everything in

and gives it back, reflecting on that moment,
sighing in insightful serious tones.

≈

I find a stone soothed by its passing.
I am reassured everything is constant and moving.

Everything is replaced.
Everything is a message for interpretation.

I dip my hands into the water, break
the sheen of surface into its translucent skin.

≈

It is strange, isn't it, how things find each other?
The alabaster water finds the land.

There is listening among the cattails. A raven
studies intently at its own reflection of dark-blue feathers.

You edge at the water waiting for it to move.
Something in me ripples when you call my name.

≈

Things are not what they seemed at first.
Reflection and new light makes things what they are.

When you reach into water, the thing you try to get
is elsewhere. Who am I to judge what is clear

or not? What is now is different. When I look again
you are still there, dissipated into rain,

hesitant as a migration searching for something better.
It is the staying that seems strange and right.

≈

A journey begins as the sun takes off,
bunches of feathers remaining in a nest of branches.

Fish strike out at small things making ripples
moving towards us. Everything moves closer.

Canoes paddle into shore, in wavering heat.
Gulls circle and lift like hearts.

What was not there before,
is there now.

HOW WE CAN CHANGE THINGS

Too often, I am aware of the land beneath my feet
and how it came to be. How it was here first,
and, how it will be here last.
As a healer, I am connected to the earth.
I feel what the earth feels. And it does not feel well.

Where has the Eastern Rosebud gone?
The Passenger Pigeon was hunted out of existence.
Where, too, are the scimitar leaves of the Honey Locus?
It used to litter the fields as reminders
that things are supposed to return.
Life is as fragile as lawn full of Baby's Breath.

What survives us?
We need to be better caretakers.
We do this forgetting
as if reality was star-shaped leaves from Sweet Gum
tossing themselves into the air.

Instead, change is a river of wind
with music, flapping tremendous wings of hope,
taking me to where I belong
over the curve of regret
to a place solemn filtered as light,
fresh as forsythia in winter, its yellow bugles
making its song of settling, waiting for me.

RETRIBUTION

Over fields of planted suburban houses,
cracking whips of frizzed blinding light,
leave patterns of shadows of our former selves
plastered temporarily on stucco walls.

Fixated on the lawn,
twisted, broken telephone wires sizzled like bacon.

Father wandered in our dazed house:
how sins were packed away in suitcases,
how no one ever sees retribution coming
until it comes.

EVERY SPRING

I pry loose wet, brown, crinkled leaves
from the downspout, a premonition of spring.
A tree's roots extend into our yard.
I section off parts of the garden
with recycled red brick. There is much to be done,
and there is no end of it. I put my foot down
on the hoe and push. I am determined
to make something of it. *This* is my demarcation line.
This is where I will grow things. The grass,
weeds, and dandelions can have the rest.
The garden hears me coming, a week away.
The ground gears-up for it.
I wish I could say the same for myself.
Someday, I will be too old for this. But for now,
I try to be up to the task, gauging myself,
sectioning off work so it is less work.
Getting older and gardening,
I have learned to spread myself
as if I had all the time in the world.

MEMORIAL TREE

Coal would rumble down a chute
into the bin that is no longer there,
black dust coughing. My mother told me,
my father had lost his hearing in the war.
I went outside searching for it.
I buried some toy German soldiers,
I dug up forty years later planting a memorial tree.
Later I found a pirate map I had drawn
showing their location. They were still green plastic,
fighting dirt, the color of coal dust.
I was up past bedtime, excavating re-call.

Someone pruned the memorial tree into nothingness,
branches empty in surrender.
I was used to speaking loudly and clearly
so my father could read lips. Now I had silence,
searching through the coughing dark;
my hands were green plastic.

Coal rumbling above, my voice so loud,
I had to remember to keep it down;
people were sleeping, far away from wars.
We all make maps of hiding places we forget about.

I was trying to summon up why I planted the tree,
who I was memorializing, what the occupation
of Normandy had to do with anything,
which pirate I wanted to be when I grew up,
why I anticipated coal delivery
with fear and anticipation, how it was deaf.

We live in our ancestry of forgetfulness
until something is retrieved like a buried toy.
Why had I blamed the green German soldier
for my father's hearing
since my father had been in the Pacific,
listening for enemy aircraft?

Sometimes, childhood makes no sense;
we prune back memories
until empty branches remain.

A STORM IS IMMINENT

The impression of calm is a lie.
A front settles like a man bringing a fist-fight.
Clouds rock on their heels, tensing before the blows.
Something intense is about to begin.

Expect the worse, and it will happen.

It is always like this before a storm —
the size of things becomes magnified.
Weather gets worse as miles grow more distant.
Then the seams of the sky split open.

What part of bad things does not happen to everyone?
When trouble comes, no one is prepared.
Clench your teeth, shiver, and wait.

Or it gets lost in the rain.
Let it drench you bone-weary.

RAIN

"He grabbed a storm out of a sea and threw it down on the canvas."
— Guy de Maupassant, about Monet

Brushstrokes of perpendicular sun-spray
splash yellow on white cove cliffs – rain
is coming; felt, rather than seen.
Degrees drop – fleeting and introverted –
then there is a hush before things happen.
What part of *this* or *anything* is ever expected?

Strange gray affects rock, cloud-rush,
gathers pitchforks of rain.
There is heaviness of air, blinding light,
before things break. There is an elusive feeling
you know what will happen next.
Premonitions come true.

Nothing penetrates.
Then, rain – echoes on waves.

Nothing is identifiable
in the downpour
from jugs of endless gray waters.
Raindrops splat into broken eggs.

We watch through a streaked window
as below, water runoffs
have nowhere to go. They coalesce.
They vacate everything in the way.
Water sieves through glass.

A storm is withering inside.

THE BEACHFRONT

>The clouds have decided not to form
>into something dramatic. Everything is
>forshortened. The seascape is slower here.
>The distance extends further than we can see.
>Two boats are abandoned on the shingle.
>The waves are static. A few sailboats
>in the coldness, are detached, in indecision,
>as to returning or turning their sails into wind.
>The air is nonchalant, willing to go wherever,
>without determination, much like us
>when we cannot make a decision.
>On the other side of the inlet
>is the spire of a church no one is attending.

SPRING

The world is estranged from itself.
In this remote area of forbidden cast-off rain-dust
and experimentally rushed-tidal plunge,
wild, primitive land-washes,
the nature of storms is studied.

We are dissatisfied with the lack of explanations.

Rocks are beaten and submerged under painful water.
Blurred white skies are not distinct from distances.
Gray monotonous clouds formulate.
Rain careens, transmitting atmosphere.
Individual areas have different amounts of rain-drench.
It rains a Debussy composition.

After rains pass, ceaseless recovery commences.

TOO SOON THE CLOUDS OF DISENCHANTED RAINS WILL BE UPON US

Too soon the clouds of disenchanted rains will be upon us
filled with reddish-orange Maple leaves
in the harvest moon-lit skies.
In that silence breathes the darkness extending into a languished sigh.
There is nothing about flowers.
There is nothing in the graying wrinkled clouds
of those brown corn stalks of light.
Too soon, the steps will turn ashen white.
If there is anything behind these closed drapes of days,
it is the knowledge things will come and go without me.
The world does not require much from me.
If I was to die tomorrow or the next, there would be no difference.
In the silence afterwards, there are flocks heading away.
In the silence after that, these are the breathless winds.
In the moments of stillness after that, there is the resting hand
upon what it means to be human, to say what is not easy to say,
to consider the long-standing stirring within us.

MARCH

It's rain-making.
Something permanent in the stone steps
is repelling rain. It stops me short,
makes me draw in my breath,
count my blessings.

It is cold, this steady rain.
But, in your heart, there, it is bristling with love.
You are writing words from March rain.
It is enough to bruise the stone of any heart.
This kind of drenching can fly
into the landscape of your bones.

EVENING SHOWER AT ATAKE AND THE GREAT BRIDGE

Based on the picture by Utagawa Hiroshige
"Mono no aware": Japanese, meaning the poignancy of transient thing

What we feel is not rain. It is the unusual
vantage point draws us towards the bridge
in the best or worse weather. This weather will clear
and return – like rice, or crabs, or plum tree blossoms.
Everything passes. New things take their place.
The bridge feels us cross before it loses its sway.
The evening will be here and gone before the rooster knows it.
I unbraid days like hair. I look back in a mirror
and tomorrow will no longer hold the same face.
Rain has nothing for me that I cannot accept.
I still need to go somewhere, or come back.
We are so short-lived. We just about begin when we end.
It is with this understanding we can deal with the largeness.
Rain falls upon us regardless if we try to shelter ourselves or not.
The lake does not have to be immense to absorb all this rain,
but it cannot contain it all if it is endlessly filling
with pregnant anguish. The bridge can only hold so much
before it gives in. Compared to the bridge, what are we?
Are we any more resilient? Can we handle any more
than we can take? What swells more: wet rice cake –
or the river of forgetfulness? What has more sadness:
the moon in its wane when it can no longer have enough light
to search for its sister, the sun – or an artist losing their sight?
What has more gratitude: the snail reaching across a yard –
or the person who knows inseparability and our deep connection
to everything? A haiku is simply a prayer. A warbler
knows more about appreciating the day better than I ever will.
I am drenched with possibilities.
What is more nourished: peonies, when the rain remembers them –
or the emptiness of the sky when birds fly in it and disappear,
reappearing elsewhere?

UNTITLED (The sky refuses to rain)

The sky refuses to rain.
For days, there is impertinence in the gust of crows
fighting over the remains.
The anguish of time is in the mother-of-pearl dawn,
where the elements are brutal as flame.
There is sorrow wherever you look.
Something wounded is looking for a place to die.
Everything is expecting things to become darker.
These are melancholy sermons.
There is an absence of prayer from the foothills.

HOW I KNOW THINGS ARE COMING BACK

Among lupines and peonies in mid-May,
there are hidden promises of the forthcoming *Astilbe*.

What is secure this season?

Double columbines of blue geraniums,
reddish-purple, tiny-leaved clematis *Etoile Violette*,
pink Japanese anemones, and large white trumpets
of *'Fragrant Cloud'*, are soloing in the chorus.
Pale white *Snow-In-Summer* spreads
on rock-edged raised beds, enjoying sunlight.

My garden is too small for my ambitions.

I have to work tight, constricted,
composing haiku of underlying colors.

If only I could've include butterscotch-gold of *Scots Pine* –
the lending of structure and intricate details,
its vessel shapes of triangle ship masts.

O what I could do with dusty-mulberry-colored *Smokebush*!

PLANTING

Planting begins in earnest,
in the most violent of snowstorms –
when clouds rub their hands with precision.

There is a constant reminder;
nothing can be planned –

from the first garden
where nothing was named,
to this garden
where nothing is too much, but it is.

SEED

1.

It took God thousands of years to learn patience;
it takes a seed a few months.

In the Silence, a whisper in your heart tells you
what to do. All you have to do is listen.

Persistence is a confession of failure
in the struggle to learn what not to do.

Things are in constant motion –
a frenzy of the making and unmaking.

I know my failures: those disquieting
malfunctions I must address them before death –

things I have discovered in meditation,
hands folded into leaves.

If I miss them, or argue with the teachings,
then I will be inside the darkness.

Who would I blame? Who will accuse me?
The soft voice resounds in my heart.

2.

What speaks? What rough tongue?
What eyes are in the clouds?
There is more than I can understand.

All the studying, all the tireless reading,
all the reciting the correct responses,
all of this and more – and still I know nothing.

I do not always hear what I need to hear.
I am small as a seed that lies unfulfilled.

3.

I am on my knees weeding, pulling the teeth of grass,
palms ingrained with dirt, digging deep in
to the dark soil, when suddenly, Light emerges!
Nothing needs to be spoken
but can be sent from heart-to-heart.

Some people do not hear anything.
They think since nothing is spoken
and since nothing more is written
and since nothing else happened,
there must be the absence of God.

Feel the pulsations of the earth.
Hear its cleansing breath.

The Presence is felt.

4.

I have planted this notion into you.
You heard me with your hands and eyes.

There is a message inside you.
Scatter it as seeds in the thrashing wind,
like magically releasing sparrows from your palms,
your heart trembling fluttering wings
lifting out of you into the infinite presence.

Every seed has a memory of what to do
what every person has forgotten.

DUTCHMAN'S BREECHES

I followed a bumblebee through early Illinois spring
to tuned-down white flowers.
I wasn't sure what I would find.

Sometimes, unplanned things are best.
I could have gotten lost, wandering like that,
in the strangeness of bee-flight.

Sometimes, you have to accept being lost
Sometimes, we see things as plainly,
and we still don't see them.

I could have been lost, and I simply did not care.
Perhaps, that lack of caring
is what made it easy to find my way back.

Burrs stuck to me,
thistles racked their pain against my hands,
and I felt no pain.

I did not care how far in or how far out I was.
Sometimes, you just have to let things just happen
in order to learn what is important.

The bees had led me to them,
in their own indirect way.
There I was, not in any hurry to get back,

and still I came back with some flowers to put in a vase
to see every aspect of them,
with the eyes of bees.

II.

SUMMER
June, July, August

ALMOND BRANCHES IN BLOOM, SAN REMY

Based on the painting *Almond Branches in Bloom, San Remy*, by Van Gogh, 1890
"There is no blue without yellow and without orange." –Van Gogh

> The white flowers indicate a sweet nut
> I devour as oceans of blue sunsets
>
> dormant during winter,
> a yellow poem waiting to bloom.
>
> The orange sun opens sunflower petals,
> yellow mist pulsates on leaves.
>
> I find a blue that is impossible,
> sighing names of things to come.
>
> The mailman could hide letters in his blue whiskers.
> Each letter opens as sparrow eggs.
>
> The orange cobblestone streets are alphabets.
> Nuns gather them into schoolchildren reciting by rote.
>
> Your words migrate into my heart.
> I am not so lonely when you write to me like this.

GARDEN HAIKUS

Hydrangeas change
between acts of a play
getting ready to perform

≈

Impatiens wait
to fill the empty garden,
wait impatiently

≈

Bees bring summer
to the creamy-peach flower
of the Almond bush

≈

A circular wall
and rain make a moat,
drawbridge to a tree.

≈

The radial structure
of the Allium, afterwards,
spikes, like frost bursts

UNTITLED (The naïveté of the day)

The naïveté of the day –
to assume I know better to do with it –
as if I was the Jay bringing its joy, or warnings.
Sometimes, blue is in the aspens,
where the far clouds flirt around.
Sometimes, blue is found as a rock
we can massage to feel its inside.
If I was able to travel anymore,
the first things I would explore would be myself,
as if I were white rapids,
as if Jays could fly out of my mouth
becoming the rocks and aspens.

CRICKETS

While planting thick, miniature, devilish gardens
of leopard-spotted ferns, there, in humbling silence,
there is an almost-sound, our ears have almost nearly forgotten.
It is so small, so easy to almost miss its faint beginnings.
It takes awhile for recognition to plant itself.
It is a secret we might have missed.

A cricket was singing thanks.

As summer heat grew fierce as penance,
the cricket sang sharper and faster.
You measure heat by its frantic clicking.
As everything cools, it slows its message.
Songs carry dawn throughout the night
as if its songs of praise were never long enough.

And after all, isn't it what this is really all about –
this singing life; this tremble of heart and heat;
chants of simple pleasures; these sublime desires,
hiding in greenness with incredibly, grateful singing.

THE CRICKET

A Cricket preaches in song.
It has one short season
to serenade the green as a lover.

And when summer is gone, a tiny silence
afterwards is the loss all lovers feel
when love is gone.

I, too, am singing my last song,
notes of green leaves,
under an open window of moonlight.

The night hears me.
It knows my bamboo-flute heart. It knows
the shortening seasons.

Music is vines, intertwining around each other,
as lovers, making cricket-noises,
surrendering to the coda of the moment.

CATARACTS

The garden is writing its messages.
Frost cracks and crackles on windows.
Swarms of birds practice flying in synch
in the papyrus of night sky.
The whimper of chimney smoke is intersected by wrens.

I miss those small spaces between your skin,
how water beads like glass snow-globes.
It is these things I want to remember
before I lose sight of everything!
Things that matter, things that count,
things that fracture the heart
into slivers of lost light.

GATHERING SHELLS

I went early to the beach,
before dark completely rendered itself useless,
when ink-blue meets pink and yellow partitions open.

After last spume of high tide had withdrawn,
its last loud lament, receding, I went to search for shells,
to see if any remained and how many.

There was disappointment. All were broken, alone,
glittering, like mica, into so many particles
that nothing remained to be identified –

only raw fish smells in cool wet sand.
I had come all this way for nothing.
Where had the souvenir shop found theirs?

I gather the decimated shells.
There is acceptance in what I had been given.
All this life-and-death is belonging and openness.

UNTITLED (The bluish butterflybush calls to me)

The bluish butterflybush calls to me.
It has nectar to taste, mash against my nose,
summer spring-mist for my hair.
I want to swim in it. Have its stickiness on my arms.
I want to be heavy with slumber and fullness,
drunk with honey, slid my tongue in like a spoon,
flute it to get the most of it, and uncoil it into my belly.
Then who would question if I sprouted feelers,
if papery wings of symmetrical spots emerged,
if I migrated to Mexico and back?

The honey locust tree would be next.

The brutal elegance of waiting
is impossible; the blossoms of music
is almost heard
from behind locked white doors.

The blunt wildness cannot hold me still.

I am a pulsating moon
flinging fields of shaggy waters.

GARDENING IN GEORGIA CLAY

I built a garden on riverbank Georgia red clay: hard dirt
used to make pottery
and not quite right for planting.

In that indeterminate soil was shale ledge, fragments
of tonsil-shaped shells, and coarse beach sand
with particles and filaments from a factory
long reduced to brick, sparkling as night full of fireflies,

I excavated, hands covered with shell-shocked fire ants
biting their discomfort. My hands became swollen
and inflamed for weeks, welded shut,
and almost palsied, stiff as a trowel.

I learned the hard facts, then: wear leather gloves
thick as determination.

The information on the seed packets
of how-to-do, what conditions and starting periods
were best and when it was too late, what zone I was in,
where does the frost stop,
when to expect if you follow instructions
carefully, how to determine failure.

After several growing seasons, after several dry seasons
when dirt clumped into afterthoughts,
after several on-going drenching seasons
when soil ran as rivulets taking everything with it
including the seeds, reason, and a watering can,
I soon knew enough of failure.

Failure followed me to work, punching out
my need to re-locate. Failure influenced the temperature
of divorce and the refusal to re-pollinate.
It washed out anything I wanted to hold onto.
It was impossible to manage as the red clay.

Yes, I know a thing or two about failure.
I also know about the joy of seeing the first sprout,
the warm wash of tomato-colored suns,
and sometimes, sometimes, the impulsive clay
was just enough to retain moisture,
just enough for the self-seeding *Forget-Me-Nots*
to remember what they were supposed to do.

And in those moments, I would remove the garden gloves,
head into the house, knowing what I had to do.

WHEN YOU LEFT ME

a cloud hunkered over a raft of water.
How do you prepare for what comes out of nowhere?
The heart is a warning bell, silent in the morning.

When you left me, things dissolved painfully.
Why must love be so ruinous and wondrous?
My window is empty, seeing nothing of you.

What we leave behind is in direct relation
to the impact of tracks, trace elements,
bone fragments, elliptical imprints on rocks.

Why do we arrive only to leave?
What holds fast? What lets go?
Are we nothing more than a ripple?

I tell you, that as long as one person remembers you,
you are still alive and count for something
more than a passing.

WILDLY PREACHING AMONG SUNFLOWERS

Van Gogh wanted to be a preacher
to spread the good word, harvesting
both field hands and the merchant,
with all the fever, with all the joy of birds,
converting everything, even the lichen.
But it was not to be.
He could not mold prayer, like a baker into bread.
He felt betrayed by his lack – his faithlessness.
His cold eye turned inward: *I am not worthy.*
He did not like what he saw. A man
whose hands wanted something other than a Bible.

He would have flogged himself,
but his weakness was that of a newborn calf.
What good were his words?
Everything was so unattainable.

He thrashed around in the fields,
wrestling with himself – and losing.
When he exhausted himself, he lay in a field of sunbursts.
Sunflowers stared with one eye, like a half-blind god,
praising him for trying. Moments of color
passed into him as sacraments.
He knew then, what he had to do.

He stumbled from one vision to another
for the next ten years, painting what he clearly saw,
even if it was disturbing, transitory, and elating.

His hands had the transformative power of sunflowers.

SEEING LIKE NEVER BEFORE

> "What have you done with your eyes?"
> — Antonio Machado

One day a thin veil lifted from my eyes.
Cherry blossom petals covered the world
in a blanket of pink whispers.
My skin felt a Presence like never before.
A swarm of crawling bees were laying honey
as bricks of dreams.
This is when poems rise out of well water, in mists.
My eyes were seeing things meant to be seen.
Now I can fall back into myself,
into a new body. One that dances.
One that has more colors than I know what to do with.

BLOODROOT

(Sanguinaria canadensis)

Those white flowers with yellow centers do not last long,
and like love, can be gone before you know it.
The trick is to enjoy it while you can.

You would think both would last longer,
but you are never surprised when they do not.
There are ways of prolonging love.

I look into your yellow pupils and repeat
what needs to be said when in love.
Three short words open things up.

Enjoy the moment while it lasts.
Let's hope it lasts longer than we expect.
Maybe I have discovered the secret after all.

EVENING

Based on the painting by Daubigny

Night is having its last fling.
Noises lessen and deepen
into old men arguing about an old tale's ending.
There is familiar and strange.
Something flies in darkness
leaving no trace of its being there at all.
Distance moves closer.
Stone walls try to hold things back.
A pond is disturbed,
then settles into old routines.

This is the way it is always is.
There is no getting used to it.
A stranger is on the highway walking home.
There is nothing to know here.
Nothing is familiar or the same here.

A stranger is walking towards what remains of light,
never reaching it fast enough.

The hills are already hunkering down.

Houses try to relax. Their floors grit and groan.
A door clatters with wind-fall, turning off the light.

Silence settles in.

THE SOUNDS OF COLORS

> "I want a red to be sonorous, to sound like a bell."
> – Pierre Augusté Renoir

There is an effect of light on an object
juxtaposes tints as to make colors alive
and quiver, as if the surface was breathing.
I often hear this, although I am losing my hearing.
I hear color altering – it is not always bells.
Sometimes, they warn like crows warring over a carcass.
Sometimes, they jangle like cow bells returning.
Sometimes, they are water snuggling against a canoe.
Sometimes, they haggle over nothing and everything
like at an open bazaar where someone is handling
a silk scarf before wearing on their head.
The sound of color speaks with authoritative words.
They converse with sensuality like a whispering lover
whose words reach inside you, tingling and joyous.
It is not always so tonally red,
although I can read the surface
easily as a capstone or an anecdote of bronze sunsets.
What should you have me make of such intensity?
Such laboring? To gain, what? – heaven?
I am deluged in their songs of praise.
And what should I not be caught up in? – the adoration?
And why should I ignore it, when I can't?
I am a newcomer to these sounds.
Or perhaps, more like a beachcomber
finding what remains when the tides recede.
When I hear what others do not, I am blessed!
And in this, I am closer to what I need to hear.
Sometimes, it is too much for just one person.
Sometimes, it just begins to be enough.
The red winds of music are bells in my heart ringing.

III.

FALL
September, October, November

SEPTEMBER

"The sickly greeny pink smile of the last flower of autumn..."
                                                    –Van Gogh

The empty stone seats and gloomy box-trees
offer no cure. The sensation of anguish
in the flight of the death-head moth
is more than I can withstand. The turbulent winds
with its quiet sadness, imagine the end of summer.
The disturbed moods of these vast passive fields
anticipates their own madness. The range of broken colors,
the improvised cold-grey skies absent of birds,
sinuous in last light, are impulsive,
diffused over strained, exhilarated hills.

NOT MARBLE NOR THE GILDED MOMENT

Based on a line from Shakespeare sonnet #55

Who best determines beauty and if it is eternal
when it is not. We are not marble in our feelings,
nor gilded in momentary thoughts.
When we are loved, nothing seems to matter.
When we feel abandoned, then it is from a marble heart,
a fool's-gold instant. There are more types of Love
then there are lovers. There is nothing more unsettling
and nothing more reassuring than Love. Nothing
separates more or connects more. What are we to do?
We are attracted and we are repelled;
we are loosened from docks, like ships without oars.
We return and are welcomed, or rejected.
We continue to fail and fail, and hope anyway. We curse
those that leave us and encourage those who accept us.
Where are you on the scales of Love?
I am not marble; I bleed. I am not in the gilded moment;
I have been hurt, and I have been in Love.
Sometimes, I am in all of them at the same time.
My voice is hoarse from proclaiming Love.

ROSE OF SHARON

Pancratium maritimum

I am sleeping on pillows of flowers
arriving as pink flamingos.

Fall is when the trimming begins.
Winter bareness drips icicles.
Then spring buds whisper your return.

The clippers hang around,
mercilessly in the shed, sharpening their skills.

ASTRONOMY LESSON ABOUT LOVE

I would like to say we share the same night star view,
but that is not true. We are more than time zones apart.
Any further away, you would not search for me.

I know you will not read this. You will tear up the envelope
once you see the zip code. Once you know it is from me,
your hatred will return, and the distance will extend further.

But isn't this fierce anger from love? Those stars
revolve regardless how you feel. You cannot stop them
any more than you can stop me from trying.

I would like to say you will get over your anger,
but this too is a lie. A black hole is swallowing truth.
When star gazing, you do not find love.

It is when you read letters from former lovers,
you find elliptical orbits. I would like to say many things,
but you would not listen, spinning away.

Futility is the curvature of the horizon,
knowing we cannot see beyond
our own need or suffering.

Love has its own gravitational pull
as well as its own course and, sometimes,
it is not going in the same direction as we are.

I would like to say a lot of things,
but they are not necessarily true.
So I say nothing. I write asteroids of letters.

I suspect that if you looked into the night sky
it would be cloudy, no moon, and empty
as mail not opened. You would not hear me.

You are going about your business, perfectly content,
while I am mooning, full of lack of gravity,
on a path that I have no control over.

How happy must be the person
who cares less about astronomy,
and cares more about the gravity of love.

REPAIRS AND MORE REPAIRS

a ladder against a house
is a man needing a crutch
about to repair
the roof of the world,
hammering all day if necessary

returning shadows to the garden,
sweeping pebbles until they glow,
going on like normal
if there is any getting back to it

ILE AUX FLEURS

Based on the painting by Monet.

There is nothing unusual about standing in wildflowers near a river.
Across the way, blue shadows of trees are thin as smokestacks.
There is nothing that moves anything, but everything is moving.

The river vibrates. The wind hums with katydids.
The clouds meander like geese heading elsewhere in no hurry.
The wildflowers stir, shaken, and flush with stillness.

There is nothing unusual about moving on.
There is nothing special to keep one here, if they are in a hurry.
There is always somewhere to go, something we have to do,

someone is waiting for us, somewhere a job we started
is still undone, a ferry boat is about to cross,
someone will miss it, there are secrets someone will whisper.

We stay. We decide to continue. It is getting late.
We agree and stay longer than we intend.
We stay and wonder why we have to go anywhere.

LETTING GO

The wildness is everywhere – old branches
break off in soft winds like loose teeth;
rocks break free of the ground where they have been
longer than memory; rivers are changing the ground around them.

This calling is passionate, shaking foundations.
We have been waiting for this calling our whole lives.
What are you waiting for? A second calling?
There might not be another moment this deep, this impulsive.
A following of this calling is a kind of necessary madness.

This is calling from a distant place.
Do you want to listen?
I do not speak of these things lightly,
for they are the directionless oars
lifting out of stilled waters.
Let the stream carry you away.
Tranquil clouds hover over as heartbeats across the sky.

How can this continue, you may wonder.
Put the oars into your boat and see where you go.

NATURE

We are immersed in nature, ceaselessly painting
with anticipation in the orchestra of wildflowers,
for those things hidden under low-lying bushes
bring forth the essence of fact –

that all things encircle us, formed by light,
in the movement of air,
whether it is still or ruffled as a river,
where everything graces our wonderment,
smells buzzing, colors soaked in dew,
transparent senses brush us,

either with winter hoarfrost, or southern heat
stretched out like a stroked cat,
or flashes of sunlight
as dragonflies in the trembling mysterious forest,
or emanating from the keening suburbs,
or from the factories leaning their smokestacks
against the fractured atmosphere –

if we ever live long enough, let us enjoy
these enflamed fluctuations of light
with trickles of indigo and absorbing blues

OCHROMA BLOSSOMS IN A RAINSHOWER

African honeybees in moonlight
unbutton the blouses of flowers
for one-night stands
causing nectar-binge from balsa tree,
there are fire ants obscured in sugary pools
oscillating like lava flows
a boa glaives in a coil of fragile rain
not interested in the white flowers
but rather in what they attract
they say things happen
in the dry season of Panama
and if you do not know what to look for
you will miss it
navigational lights in the distance
lead nobody to nothing

THE FOREST IS AS FAR OR AS NEAR AS YOU WANT IT TO BE

1.

things there are at a better place –
a sanctuary of pines, sumac,
silver maple, moss-sided trunks
smooth as wafers of light –
a shrine of holy voices.

2.

It is not always about fleshy beginnings
or renewals. There is death,
same as anywhere else,

and like anywhere else,
death cannot help being there.

3.

Death comes for all things –
a solemn version of ready-or-not
taps you on the shoulder.
Things give up, ripen, and rot.

We never always see it coming –
the mystery of it.
We bury ourselves
in the fullness of what's-next.

THE RIVER OF FORGETFULNESS

Note: It is one of the five rivers of the Greek underworld.

There are things we wish we can forget.
There are things we put so deeply into ourselves
we forget that they are there. Memory is a river
without a bridge. It remembers dark things.
The current of the mind is too swift
to swim across. We can only wish
for things to be different. But they are not.

After a war, some of us return,
but we never make it back.
Some of us return wounded,
a body part missing,
and we see things
we never want to talk about.
It is river to nowhere.

We want to bath in that water,
drink endlessly, carry it in canteens.
Instead, we are on a ferry boat,
as the shore keeps pulling further away.

MESSAGE

The ascending flat needles on the Balsam Fir;
the loose, irregular, feathery needles of the Hemlock;
the shaggy leaves of the Cottonwood;
and the flat sprays of Northern White Cedar
are all I can see.

If something were to happen to me
and I was taken away from all of this,
the forest would remain
long after I was gone.

I know I am going soon.
I hear it from a Yellow Warbler hanging in branches
of Lombard Poplar. Its crisp music remains there,
slender in those continuous branches.

The Warbler flies into tomorrow
taking news to others –
they will be leaving too.

AFTER

A hawk takes its noise into the temporal sky,
spiraling as resonance disappears.

This is a part of darkness.
We are attracted to the possibility of death.

We watch, curious. We carry this emptiness
for hours as we try to understand and forget.

It fades with the cry, into the nothingness,
funneling a heartbeat into the beyond.

The hawk leaves and is replaced
by something more trembling than awareness.

TOUCH IS SOMETHING WE ALL NEED

"I love pictures which make me want to stroll in them, if they are landscapes, or caress them, if they are nudes." – Pierre Augusté Renoir

Better yet, I want to caress a landscape.
I want the impact of the translation of light
upon the waves ingrained on a tree bark,
and I want to trace my fingers on those deep furrows
to hear what they have seen all those watchful years.
It is the same as massaging and breaking the tension
like a rise of startled quail, or the break of air at sunrise.
In that tree's branches, trying to hold things still
long enough for us to enjoy seeing them:
a song of a pinfeather, a knit of string and sprigs,
a egg holding its secrets in blue-speckled breathes.

Below, flowers curl as earlobes,
hearing things approach,
waiting for us to inspect them for perfection –
like a craftsman with absolute standards.
I want to stroke across the chambers,
like soft-carpeted footsteps
approaching a lover, as if I want to touch
the light in their hair before it fades
and find the undertones.

In the naked light,
everything looks like field sprays,
like dappled skin in transferred light,
like it has been waiting all morning
for us to kiss them with the lightest kiss possible,
not waking up or startling anything,
and still be a kiss. It is waiting for us to find it –
in this exposed moment, that is,
if we are not too embarrassed to look.

Look!
– it is blushing as a rose petal in the arousal of light.
How it purrs and stretches, satisfied,
as it slides into awakening.

IV.

WINTER
December, January, February

TRILLIUMS

Trillium grandiflorum

When we age, something changes,
like the trilliums, from papery-white to pink.

My slippers scuffle across the floor.
I count pills and vitamins, wondering
which is supposed to slow down illness.
Where did these age spots come from?
What happen to that carefree boy?
Who is that stranger in the mirror?
Why is he mocking me?

If you pick trilliums, you destroy the whole plant.
It takes a year for them to recover.
Ever since my body turned papery-white,
it is taking longer for me to recuperate too.
These pills do nothing.
I have no confidence in them.
I seem to get worse as they increase.

Trillium seeds are spread by ants.
Where are the ants for me?
The one thing I have in common with trilliums
is when they mature, they turn soft and spongy.
There is no comfort in knowing they can cure bleeding.
There is no comfort in knowing anything.

There is only comfort in finding them in the fields
thinking they have opened for me
just when I needed comfort most.

When we age, something changes.

TRACE EVIDENCE

1.

There is a moment, in darkness,
when dark changes, as it hesitates,
trying to resist daybreak, shimmers,
purple as a bruise, losing the fight.

This last black-upon-shaded-black
is when clouds start to become noticeable.
The horizon is differentiated from shaping trees.
It is when all things give way to other things.

What was hidden is emerging.

We can begin to see where land begins and sky ends.
Light is still taking its time getting here.
But it is coming – at its own cumbersome pace.

All things must change –
like a battered rush of crackles changing directions.

Those impulsive birds make a clap
as they rise
pulling pink snails of light into the sky.
Leaves darken with green light,
no longer blending with hills.

We wake to an alarm clock of cicadas.

There is a fundamental sameness and differences.
Yellow-redness is the last thing of morning,
as drawstrings lift dark.

2.

When the sun ascends the ladder of hills,
is it replaced in the absence of evidence?

Where are you in this darkness?
This beginning light?
What trace evidence of yourself is left behind?

If you say you did the same thing today as yesterday,
you would be wrong.

No matter how mundane we are, or think we are,
we never have the same experience every day.
For every single day, things are happening.

Send out evidence you care.
Send out evidence, that in the end, we are evidence.
Ascend the rugged ladder of hills as a morning song,
using a lantern of moon.

WHAT WILL HAPPEN IF WE PULL DOWN THE EMPTY SKY

Dreams would crash on our heads,
all those prayers we felt went nowhere,
would fall on us as meteorites.
Some people would deny this,
even though they would see it with their own eyes,
for this is the way of things unexplained.
A preacher would say it was predicted in the Bible,
when it was clearly not there.
Someone would lose a house
and discover it is not covered by insurance,
and it turns out that person sells insurance.

This is what happens when we let things go,
when we find more ways to kill each other,
when we sleep in our comfortable bed while
things go haywire.

And the sky itself would be missing.
The nightmares will begin.

Sleep while you can.
The days of reckoning are not here yet.
This is not a final warning.
The pillars are still supporting the weight of the sky.

Beware of the politicians who are like woodpeckers
chipping at the ways things should be
until the sky finally does fall on our heads.
The ones with the sharpest beaks
are the ones most dangerous.
You will know them by how sleepless they make us
with their constant loud noise tapping at reality
in order to get their way. Hear them?
They are the ones who make us irritable enough
to hurt strangers. They are the ones who only care
for things that are destroyed from the outside in.

UNTITLED (The dictionary of clouds opens to the section about awakening)

The dictionary of clouds opens to the section about awakening –
shutters flapping in wind. The heat index rises to unbearable,
while we formulate the next impossible question.

Things are being written. Nothing changes.
The outcome fractures its lungs. The sun seeks comfort,
burying itself in mud, like a frog.

Birds lose their song.
Things dry up, vacant as the sky.
Clouds are drained into nothing.

LASTING

A final dark-spotted leaf
is folding its mystery in purple, still attached
to branch trying to shake it loose
into crunching fallen colors, brittle in air.

It did not want to let go – dying
and resurrecting into its next stage.
Dirt was under some leaves, loving the fall.
The leaf clung to what it knew.

It did not want to go into the unknown.
Soon, it would have no choice. It would be gone.
I, too, would be gone. My staying is not possible.
My returning to the soil is welcomed and waiting.

My heart is straight with the universe.
For some, it is the end. For me – what a beginning!
In the excellence of seasons and weather,
we cannot change inevitability. We can only embrace it.

HIROSHIMA

August 6, 1945

During the bomb

blackened skeletons of houses
smoldering shoulders of gray smoke
boiling air

not that a warning would have helped
or made a difference

bad karma strikes indiscriminately

it does not care what it wallops
as long as it inflicts as pain

After

there is no difference between
holding a hand and letting go

speak for the dying

the day is being repaired for some
and ending for others

stretch me out on a stretcher of tongues

≈

When my wife died, my hands were empty
and did not know what to do

I hammered
trying to repair what was broken

I would like to say it was my carelessness that made her die,
but I had no more control of our lives
than the random smacking of nail with a hammer

I would like to say, if I had spent more time that last minute
telling her what I want to say now,
I would have said everything I needed to say

None of this matters when you have no control

It is not like repairing missing tiles on a roof
or hammering
until your arms have more pain than your heart,
one kiss is one more thing in a world of nothing

Things have a way of happening
when they are meant to happen:
no matter how much we try to understand
we never do

No matter what we try to repair, it takes awhile

≈

the names of the dead
written on paper lanterns
float on the Ohita River
to endless waters of the sky

countless paper lanterns
offer stories
about to extinguish

know this:

write my name
on the skin of the paper,
set a match to it,

send it down the river,
recite my name
until your lips are numb,
carry my story
as a swaying paper lantern

~

the earth can only handle so much grief
before it tears out clumps of hair, retching
blood no bandage can heal

nothing looks clean
the earth is dark as a broken clay pot
someone has thrown away

no breeze can cool this off

FLORIDA, FROST SEASON

Dawn ignites an empty bell.
No one hears it. Not me. Not you.
A quiet mystery hangs oranges in the grove.
What will survive? Leaves turn brittle.

More has to be said about loss.
Aimless tides of frost arrive.
This is the deathless way.
If things fail, they fail quickly.

It is too late.
The orchards are frosting over,

You know what to do.
The fruit is not ready for the crates.
We can lose everything,
but that is not what is important.
What is important is us,
what we mean to each other.
We are more than pickers of fruit.
If we have no faith in ourselves, we have nothing.

The sun is dripping ice crystals.

I am leaving you to all of this.
You know where to find me.
I will be dying, one brittle leaf at a time.

AFTER WINTER

        The decayed leaves on browned
        field-covers under spines
        of trees, near tuffs of spiked grass
        is purple torques of crocus;
        things are fighting to return
        in limited space

        glacier rocks are fisted up,
        freckled with lichen and moss,
        splashed with remains of tattered snow

        things struggle to be recognized,

        they break through, thirst for light,
        as the mountains continue to move
        ongoing and ponderous,
        over hundreds, thousands,
        hundreds of thousand years

        everything is restless.

DURING A LONG JOURNEY

The road becomes hypnotic,
speaking of things that are passing;
like sirens, about things pass due,
like how leaves are collected into soil,
like the clouds take away and give.

You are tight as hands on a steering wheel.

You pull over to rest.
You let the world rush by you
like a flight of restless birds.

You lower the side window.
A breeze from somewhere distant, visits.
It has been waiting just for you.
It always has been waiting for you.

It takes awhile to relax
into the heartbeat around you.
Some things should never be hurried.
Like a seed that takes time
in silent prayer before awakening.

You are under a tree.
You start to wonder what kind of tree it is.
But the name relaxes within you.
You let go of something,
then you let go of everything.
And then the day turns its page on you.

EXTINCTION

The saddest word is *extinction*.
No more of a species will be born;
none will be seen except in old photographs;
they will not be vibrant. It is the eradication
of rebirth and continuation. None is absolute.
What part of this loss cannot touch God?
What loss is replaced? What is rending open?
How will it be spoken, and will it be speechless?

When the last Beech was removed,
it affected the Passenger Pigeon
who had carried its seed.
So pigeons fell in clusters out of the sky
into the nothingness.

What other things will disappear,
causing the demise of others?
And when, oh when, will this loss reach us?
What terror will finally befall us?

A warning unheard is the second saddest word.

REACHING US

Breathing first starlight is the same
as a white peach stone, knife
edge on whet stone to hone it
to match the skills it will need,
is the same as
blue irises,
the harmonics of the green apple
in the yellow room,
the loom of light and the shadow
woven by the spider, is the same as
impaired vision, loss of smell,
the caged vocabulary releasing itself –
that which goes beyond hesitation
is that which searches like a pelican
trying to fill its bill in an depleted area.
Things may take a thousand years to reach us,
but they do with clarity.

SINGING IN THE APRON OF STARS

I did it. I sang full-throttle
while the neighbors glared suspiciously,
and it felt *right*, annoyingly right,

the word *"proper"* did not fit into the scales,
nor *"consideration"* for melody or harmony,
or if the words were well chosen,
or if anyone listened to me,

I was liberated, for even a moment,
to do what my heart knew instinctually right,
and I was doing what I should be doing

I was clipping the hedges with hymns

Caterwauling, one neighbor judged,
but I could not help it,
I could not bear my silence anymore
and I needed to join the choir of nightingales
singing well past bedtime
into the apron of stars

I could not help it; my longing was so great,
so impetuous, I could not stop the ocean of song,
nothing could stop me, not dusk,
not coal-dust night

my throat came down with laryngitis,
until I croaked from my swollen belly

I sang, even in my sleep,
on bed sheets of music
beyond and into the A cappella of new mornings.

ON THE TERRACE

> Based on the painting by Renoir, 1879
> "I arrange my subject as I want." – Renoir

We are portrayed for more than we are.
Light gathers in a sewing basket.

She is about to stitch sunbursts
into coneflowers. She can find rest here,
waiting to overflow into the background.
How simple, simple is.

We may never sit against a balustrade;
but we can almost experience the feel of it
against our back, almost feel the fields behind,
almost feel wind against our cheek,
soft as a skein of yellow sighs.

We are all in this moment.

We can almost sense that girl
peeking from the edge, lifting on her toes.

How simple, simple is.
Vines intertwine fences,
sun interlaces with shadow,
trees become shapes of disarming simplicity.
How we try to arrange things!
We should arrange them as simple statements
about the simplest of messages
like yellow flowers in a basket.

CANADA GEESE

The noisy beginnings, the leaving stretching the sky,
the interminable returns,

they come & depart in an right angle taking the treetops off
as a wedge into a last echoed song,

this ritual happens twice yearly, never the same, never
changing, always knowing when the change is coming

they announce this change, breaking the icy clouds,
like laying eggs, like hatchlings breaking free in taps & cracks,

they remember what we forget:
things are the same & different, always in flight, always nesting,

we cannot lift out of our bodies, nor see the land slowly below us,
nor call the changing of the seasons so it will change like they can,

this is how love begins, the calling & responding,
this is how we should migrate & mate, and dip into water,

taking turns leading & following so neither tires,
in a formation of co-operation so none are left behind

THREE HOURS BEFORE NEW YEARS AND COUNTING

I knew that New Years Day was off to a bad start
when snow began to fall inside of my closet,
geese flew from the coat hangers,
and someone tobogganed out of the shoe boxes.
I could blame the Mayan calendar
for predicting the end of the world,
but the sun just rose over New Zealand
and it will take hours by bus transfer to get here.
Where is my party hat for the chaos coming at tax time?
Does it mean anything that the Saint Bernard
is bringing an application to AA?
The Walrus brought his own bucket of ice for the Champagne.

THINGS WE FIND INSTEAD OF OTHER THINGS

Winding overgrown paths with raw, tempered cliffs
are accidental findings.
A spring, the size of a tree stump, ripples like tree rings.

This is where words are easy to forget.
Thoughts are things left behind.

Some things need time to study, to take it all in, before it vanishes.
Start where impetuous noises end, and work from there.
Night will anchor soon.

Wait for things to arrive that never seem to arrive.

The sun will climb the ridgeline.
There is nothing to be done about it.

Take a pen with you, and write what you see in your heart.
Outwait the departing paths.

The summit we approach
is astounded into a loon,
carrying its strangeness with it.

There are things we never get to.
There are other things we find instead.
I am always searching the source of things.
I will not find it today or any other day.

That is the problem with seeking.
Sometimes, we do not find what we want to find,
and we find other things instead.
There is always something in the nothingness.

Wild winds thin out into smells from apple blossoms.

I am always wondering
what is just beyond.

ACKNOWLEDGEMENTS

Bagel Bards · "Trace Evidence"
Be About It · "Gardening in Georgia Clay"
Big City Lit · "Too Soon the Clouds of Disenchanted Rains Will Be Upon Us"
Blast Furnace · "The bluish butterflybush calls to me"
Blue Fifth Review · "Searching For What Is Not There"
Cherry Blossom Review · "Repairs and More Repairs," "Garden Haiku"
Flutter · "Untitled (the naiveté of the day)," "On the Terrace"
Hotmetalpress.net · "Hiroshima"
In Terra Pax (Cinnamon Press anthology, 2011) · "The Sounds of Color," "Touch Is Something We All Need," "During a Long Journey"
Meadowland Review · "Memorial Tree"
Our Day's Encounter · "Three hours Before New Years and Counting"
Parting Gifts · "Untitled (The sky refuses to rain)," "Ochroma Blossoms in a Rainshower," "Not Marble nor the Gilded Moment"
Punkin House (slumber theme) · "The River of Forgetfulness," "What Will Happen If We Pull Down the Empty Sky"
Red Ochre Review · "After Winter"
Red Poppy Review · "Seeing Like Never Before"
Seven Circles Press · "Retribution," "Almond Branches in Bloom," "The Beachfront"
The Stray Branch Litmag · "Reaching Us"
Tipton Poetry Review · "Canada Geese"
Voices from Everywhere (Anthology in Belgium) · "Seed"
Walnut Literary Review · "September"
Wilderness House Literary Review · "Singing in the Apron of Stars," "Cataracts," "Every Spring," "Trilliums," "Dutchman's Breeches," "Bloodroot," "Lasting"

～

"Canada Geese" was reprinted in *The Visitors & other stories & poems* (Cinnamon Press anthology)

～

"On the Terrace" was nominated for a *Best of the Net* award by *Flutter Press*, 2012.

ABOUT THE AUTHOR

MARTIN WILLITTS JR is a retired Librarian living in Syracuse, New York. He currently evaluates Prior Learning Evaluations for SUNY Empire State College. He was nominated for 5 *Pushcart* and 4 *Best of the Net* awards. He provided his hands-on workshop "How to Make Origami Haiku Jumping Frogs" at the *2012 Massachusetts Poetry Festival*. He won the *William K. Hathaway Award for Poem of the Year 2012*. He is the winner of the inaugural 2013 Wild Earth Poetry Contest for his full length collection *Searching for What Is Not There* (Hiraeth Press).

His print chapbooks include *Falling In and Out of Love* (Pudding House Publications, 2005), *Lowering Nets of Light* (Pudding House Publications, 2007), *The Garden of French Horns* (Pudding House Publications, 2008), *Baskets of Tomorrow* (Flutter Press, 2009), *The Girl Who Sang Forth Horses* (Pudding House Publications, 2010), *Van Gogh's Sunflowers for Cezanne* (Finishing Line Press, 2010), *Why Women Are A Ribbon Around A Bomb* (Last Automat, 2011), *Protest, Petition, Write, Speak: Matilda Joslyn Gage Poems* (Matilda Joslyn Gage Foundation, 2011), *Secrets No One Wants To Talk About* (Dos Madres Press, 2011), *How to Find Peace* (Kattywompus Press, 2012), *Playing The Pauses In The Absence Of Stars* (Main Street Rag, 2012), *No Special Favors* (Green Fuse Press, 2012),), and *Late All Night Sessions with Charlie "the Bird" Parker and the Members of Birdland, in Take-Three* (A Kind Of a Hurricane Press, ebook, 2013).

He has three full length books *The Secret Language of the Universe* (March Street Press, 2006), and *The Hummingbird* (March Street Press, 2009), and *The Heart Knows, Simply, What It Needs: Poems based on Emily Dickinson, her life and poetry* (Aldrich Press, 2012).

Martin Willitts Jr forthcoming poetry books include *Waiting for the Day to Open Its Wings* (UNBOUND Content), *Art Is the Impression of an Artist* (Edgar and Lenore's Publishing House), and *Swimming in the Ladle of Stars* (Kattywompus Press).

Hiraeth Press

❡ Poetry is the language of the Earth — not just poems but the slow flap of a heron's wings across the sky, the lightning of its beak hunting in the shallow water; autumn leaves and the smooth course of water over stones and gravel. These, as much as poems, communicate the being and meaning of things. Our publications are all poetry, whether they are poems or nonfiction, and reflect the ideal that falling in love with the Earth is nothing short of revolutionary and that through our relationship to wild nature we can birth a more enlightened vision of life for the future. We are passionate about poetry as a means of returning the human voice to the polyphonic chorus of the wild.

www.hiraethpress.com

CPSIA information can be obtained at www.ICGtesting.com
Printed in the USA
BVOW05s1934210115

384378BV00002B/7/P